Pau ✔ KU-286-744

A·B·H   A·M·H

First Published in 1971 by
Macdonald and Company
(Publishers) Limited
St. Giles House
49-50 Poland Street
London W1

Chief Editor
Angela Sheehan B.A.

© Macdonald and Company
(Publishers) 1971

SBN 356 03670 7
MFL 22

Made and printed in Great Britain
by A. Wheaton & Company
Exeter Devon

MACDONALD FIRST LIBRARY

Pirates and Buccaneers

Macdonald Educational
49-50 Poland Street
London W1

early pirate ship

Long ago, men set out in ships to trade with
other countries.
Sometimes sea-robbers attacked them and
stole their ships and goods.
These robbers were called pirates.
Pirate ships were light and fast.
They could easily catch up with ships carrying
heavy cargo.

Many pirates sailed in the Mediterranean Sea.
They attacked Roman ships.
They captured Julius Caesar, a Roman
emperor.
The Romans had to pay the pirates to set him
free.
When he was free, Julius Caesar found the
pirates and killed them.

Julius Caesar

The fiercest pirates lived in Cilicia beside the Mediterranean Sea.
Soon trading ships were too frightened to sail in the Mediterranean.

Roman fleets sailed to fight the pirates.
The Romans were defeated.

The Cilicians seized ships taking corn from
Egypt to Rome.
Soon the Romans were almost starving.
They set off again to fight the pirates.
They fought for many months.
In the end the pirates fled from the seas.

Years later new pirates arrived in the Mediterranean. They were called Saracens.
At first the Saracens were 'land' pirates.
They attacked and robbed cities and towns.
We call this 'plundering'.

Saracens

The Saracens soon ruled over many islands and parts of north Africa.
They sailed to Spain and captured many Spanish towns.

At the same time more pirates, called Vikings,
plundered the coasts of Britain and France.
They arrived in their terrifying dragon ships.
They robbed, burned and killed.
The Vikings liked Britain better than their
own snowy country in the north.
They stayed in Britain and became farmers.

Vikings

Many years later the Saracens were thrown out of Spain.
They became sea-pirates.
The Saracen sea-pirates were called the Barbary Corsairs.
Even brave sailors were afraid of them.

The Barbary Corsairs made their home in Algiers in North Africa.
They attacked ships carrying rich cargo.
Then they returned with the stolen goods, or 'booty', to Algiers.
They were safe from their enemies there.

Barbarossa

Their leader was called Barbarossa.
The word Barbarossa means 'red beard'.
He was killed in a battle with the Spanish.
The Spanish beat the pirates but they did not
destroy Algiers.

Ali Pasha

Another famous pirate
was Ali Pasha.
Ali Pasha was a Moslem.
He plundered Christian
ships.

The Christians sent Don
John of Austria to fight
Ali Pasha.
In 1571, they fought a
fierce battle at Lepanto.

They fought in ships
called galleys.
Don John did not have as
many galleys as Ali
Pasha, but the Christians
fought bravely.

Battle of Lepanto

The galleys rammed each other.
Men jumped onto enemy ships and fought on
the decks.
The Moslems' slaves were Christians.
They were rowing the galleys.
They began to fight against their masters.
The Moslems lost two hundred ships and
thousands of their men.

The most famous pirates lived in the time of
Queen Elizabeth I.

Hawkins and Frobisher robbed Spanish ships.
They also plundered cities on the Spanish
Main beside the Caribbean Sea.
They brought home the stolen Spanish gold.

Sir Martin Frobisher

Sir Francis Drake

The greatest
'pirate' of all was
Francis Drake.
Spain hated him.
In England he
was a hero.
He sailed home with
ships full of Spanish
gold, silver and jewels.
The Queen called him
her 'little pirate'.
She made him
a knight.

Other English sailors fought against pirates.

The new Barbary Corsairs plundered many English ships.
Admiral Robert Blake fought against them.

First he attacked the pirates in Tunis in North Africa.
Blake's powerful guns destroyed the walls of the pirates' fort.
Then he sank their galleys in the harbour.

14   Admiral Robert Blake

Then Blake sailed to Algiers.
The ruler of Algiers had already heard of
Blake's victory at Tunis.
He was so scared that he set all his British
prisoners free.
Blake took them back to Britain.
Blake did not destroy Algiers.
Pirates stayed there over a hundred years.

Henry Morgan was a famous 'buccaneer'.
When he was a young boy he was kidnapped
and taken to the West Indies.
He was sold as a slave.
When he grew up he joined a band of pirates,
or 'buccaneers', in Jamaica.
These buccaneers plundered Spanish towns
and returned with their booty to Jamaica.

Once Morgan captured the Spanish town of
Panama and killed many people.
Although they were enemies, England and
Spain were not at war.
The Spanish were very angry.
Morgan was arrested and brought to England.
But he was not punished.
The king made him a knight.

Henry Morgan at Panama

Avery

'Long Ben' Avery went to
sea with the Merchant
Navy.
He revolted against his
captain and took
command of the ship.
He sailed to the coast of
India.
He joined two pirate
ships there.
They attacked a big ship,
carrying gold and jewels.
The daughter of the
Grand Mogul of India
was also on board.
The pirates set her free.
They took the gold and
jewels.

Avery tricked the other pirate captains.
They put all the treasure in his ship.
Avery escaped with all the booty.
When he tried to sell the jewels, the buyers
cheated him.
A pirate could not complain to the police!

William Kidd

William Kidd was born in Scotland.

At first he was an honest sailor.

He was sent to fight pirates on the coast of America.

He quarrelled with one of his crew and killed him.

He was scared he would be punished.

So he became a pirate.

Kidd's pirate ship was
called the 'Adventure'.
He captured a treasure
ship.
He buried the treasure
on an unknown island
near America.

Kidd became famous as a
pirate.
He was wanted for many
crimes.
He sailed to Boston and
was arrested.
Kidd was found guilty of
'piracy' and was hanged.

Blackbeard

Edward Teach had a big bushy beard.
People called him 'Blackbeard'.
He carried six pistols.
He stuck special matches in his hat to make himself look fierce.
His cruelty soon made him the most famous pirate on the Spanish Main.
He stole a French ship.
He called it 'Queen Anne's Revenge'.
He sailed along the coast of Cuba.

He sank many ships and left their crews on
lonely islands.
The English sent the 'Pearl' to capture him.
Blackbeard jumped onto the deck of the
'Pearl'.
The commander stood waiting.
They fought fiercely.
Blackbeard was killed.

Bartholomew Roberts

Bartholomew Roberts was a strange pirate.
Most pirates drank a lot of rum or wine.
Roberts drank only tea!
He was a very strict captain.
His crew had to put out their lights by eight
o'clock.
On Sundays he read to them from the Bible.
He wore beautiful clothes.

Roberts sailed along the coast of Africa.
He captured many rich ships.
Then a British ship saw Roberts sailing
towards them.

The sailors expected a
fierce fight.
But Roberts was killed
and his crew surrendered.

Anne Bonney

Mary Read

Anne Bonney was Irish.
She lived in America.
She wanted an adventure.
She met a bold pirate.
He wore striped trousers.
He was called 'Calico Jack'.
Anne put on sailor's clothes and joined his crew.
Anne found another girl on the ship.
She was called Mary Read.
She had run away from home to join the Navy.
Then she had become a soldier.

Mary fought in France.
Then she joined Calico
Jack's crew.
Mary and Anne became
friends.
They fought side by side.
At last their ship was
captured by the Navy.
Mary and Anne were set
free.
But Calico Jack was a
coward.
He hid during the fight.
He was hanged.
Anne cried, "If you had
fought like a man you
need not have been
hanged like a dog!"

Mary Read fights a duel

Many trading ships sailed to the Far East.
They often sailed through the Straits of
Malacca between Malaya and Sumatra.
Pirates waited there for trading ships.
Malayan traders sailed in small 'prahus'
with sails.
The pirate 'prahus' had lots of oars.
They were very fast.

Malayan trading prahu

A British fleet sailed against the Malayan pirates in 1849.

One hundred and fifty pirate prahus attacked them.

An armed steamer was in the British fleet.

It frightened the pirates.

A battle began but the pirates fled.

More than half the pirate boats were caught.

Many Chinese pirates sailed from Hong Kong.
Then the island of Hong Kong became British.
The pirates all had to leave.
But they stayed in the seas around China.
They captured many ships.
At last British gunboats found them.
The British attacked the pirates bravely.
The British guns sank all the pirate ships.

Not long ago, pirates still sailed near China.
They pretended to be passengers on a ship.
They hid their guns.
When the ship was out at sea they held up the officers and crew.
This is called hijacking.
It can still happen!

Chinese hijacking

Index

MACDONALD FIRST LIBRARY

Some pirate flags